SELECTED

TO

SUFFER

SELECTED

TO

SUFFER

JIM GOOD

Tate Publishing & Enterprises

Selected to Suffer
Copyright © 2010 by Jim Good. All rights reserved.

No part of this publication may be reproduced, stored in a retrieval system or transmitted in any way by any means, electronic, mechanical, photocopy, recording or otherwise without the prior permission of the author except as provided by USA copyright law.

Scripture quotations taken from the New American Standard Bible Update, Copyright © 1960, 1962, 1963, 1968, 1971, 1972, 1973, 1975, 1977, 1995 by The Lockman Foundation. Used by permission. All rights reserved.

The opinions expressed by the author are not necessarily those of Tate Publishing, LLC.

Published by Tate Publishing & Enterprises, LLC
127 E. Trade Center Terrace | Mustang, Oklahoma 73064 USA
1.888.361.9473 | www.tatepublishing.com

Tate Publishing is committed to excellence in the publishing industry. The company reflects the philosophy established by the founders, based on Psalm 68:11,
"The Lord gave the word and great was the company of those who published it."

Book design copyright © 2010 by Tate Publishing, LLC. All rights reserved.
Cover design by Amber Gulilat
Interior design by Joey Garrett

Published in the United States of America

ISBN: 978-1-61663-097-3
Religion / Christian Life / Inspirational
10.04.27

ACKNOWLEDGMENTS

There is no greater purpose or honor than serving the Lord. Thank you, Lord, for letting me serve you.

TABLE OF CONTENTS

Introduction	9
Background	13
Loneliness	19
Stress	23
Fear	29
Patience	35
Obedience	39
Courage	45
Faith	51
Trust	59
Loss	65
Importance of Tithing	71
Dare	77
Power of Prayer	85
Importance of Timing	95
The Only Way	101
A Final Thought	111

INTRODUCTION

As I entered a parking lot at a shopping plaza, the steering wheel begged for mercy as I gripped it with manic strength fueled by rage and frustration. I had reached a point of despair and felt an overwhelming need to pull over to battle the Lord.

You see, for decades my life represented endless problems. When looking left, problems. When looking right, problems. When looking up, down, forward, and behind, yep, you guessed it, problems.

These problems came in most formats: financial, emotional, relational, spiritual, and physical.

"How dare you give me so many hardships and such little joy," I screamed at the Lord after parking. "You are nothing but a bully! Do you take pleasure in beating an orphan?"

A few more emotion-laden, choice words followed. Then a few more.

During my rant, spittle splattered the dashboard, while my hands alternated between balled fists of rage and finger-pointing accusations heavenward. My blood pressure reached heights of danger. When done ranting, a smug grin plastered my mug. I felt good. Vindicated.

"I've got him," I crowed as I started the engine and drove away. "I'm right. He can't deny anything I said."

Wrong.

Not even a minute later, the Lord spoke to my inner being.

"Jim, I watched my son, Jesus Christ, get severely beaten and flogged and then die a brutal, brutal death on the cross, and I was with him. And, Jim, you are my son too, and I'm always with you."

Rage fled. Fists released their death grip on the aching, innocent steering wheel and my blood pressure cooled.

Tears flowed.

Here I had come to the Lord with accusations, anger, frustration, resentment, name-calling, and finger-pointing—a street fighter pulling out a razor blade—yet he responded with loving-kindness, compassion, understanding, and empathy.

Love.

My thick skull then realized that no matter my situation or circumstance, the Lord lives inside me and guides and protects me. All the adversity, all the neverending problems and Goliaths blocking my way represent stepping-stones to greater heights. Once I overcome each test and trial, the Lord moves me closer to becoming a greater instrument to further his purpose.

I realized that the Lord carefully orchestrated my life to bring him eventual glory. It's about him, not me.

I realized I was selected to suffer, just like Jesus Christ.

And so are you.

BACKGROUND

I first realized as a boy that my life wouldn't be easy. My feelings of self-consciousness, insecurity, and inferiority began around age seven—way too young to worry about such nonsense.

I suffered from vitiligo, a painless skin condition that left large patches of white skin on my feet, legs, arms, and hands. I got used to the jokes and questions but not the continuous stares.

Also, I was skinny. Ribs and bones jutted, adding to my agony.

I am the middle child of three, which brought problems of its own. You middle children out there understand that albatross. But, hey, we'll leave those gripes for the psychiatrist's couch.

My father died of a brain tumor when I was twelve. I watched my once-healthy, strong father wither to emaciated proportions. About two years later, my mother remarried. My stepfather murdered her not long after the marriage. Although not exactly sure of specifics, we believe he pushed her off a bridge, and then when the fall didn't kill her, he jumped in the water and drowned her.

After the murder, upon insistence by relatives who knew something was amiss, my brother, sister, and I fled to our grandparents. My grandfather suffered from severe Alzheimer's disease at the time. We couldn't afford outside help, and my grandmother cared for him as best she could. Years later, he choked to death at the dinner table.

After we left, my stepfather changed the locks on the house my parents built and sold most of our household possessions at a public auction. I recall us picketing the auction with signs, asking buyers not to purchase our possessions but mostly to no avail.

My stepfather then sold my home. He even cashed the life insurance policy he took out on my mother weeks before her murder. I received none of those profits. He had not yet been brought to justice, and thus remained a free man, allowed to do what he wanted.

It took approximately fifteen years to convict him, including four trials: a civil wrongful death suit and three federal murder trials. We were awarded $500,000 in the civil suit, but were never able to collect a penny. Next came the federal trials. He was found guilty in all three, but let loose to silly technicalities in the first two.

Finally, after all those years of being a free man, he was justifiably thrown in prison.

He died alone in his prison cell.

I lost what seemed like everything. My father. My mother. My home. My youth. My inheritance. My sense of security.

A modern-day Job.

Due to those many more-than-stressful events, mental repercussions became my bedmate. Well into my adult years, I felt like a worthless punching bag and suffered from emotional problems, including abandonment, rejection, and trust issues.

I had been emotionally beaten to the point where I couldn't look anyone in the eyes. Whether stares at my mottled skin when younger or stares of pity and sadness after my parents' deaths, I soon attributed people looking at me as something negative. Therefore, I wouldn't lock eyes with others.

After all, I was a nobody, nothing orphan. Well, at least that's how I felt. I felt unworthy and unwanted, like stinky fish in yesterday's garbage. Man, life stunk more than that fish.

Until one day...

Driving through tiny Bowersville, Ohio, one day, I noticed a sign that read, "Birthplace of the Reverend Norman Vincent Peale." I had never heard of the chap and jokingly thought that maybe he was some hick who used to preach to cows in barns. Or maybe he held the county's distance record for tobacco spitting.

Regardless, days later, something kept nagging at me to look him up in the library. I didn't want to though, as he was a reverend and I had no need for religious nonsense. However, grudgingly, yet evermore curious, I checked out one of Norman Vincent Peale's books. Well, I quickly learned that he wasn't an ignorant hick at all. Norman Vincent Peale wrote many books about the power of positive thinking. He taught me how to change my life by changing my thoughts through Jesus Christ and biblical scripture.

For example, when a negative thought entered my mind, I learned to immediately replace it with a positive thought. Over time, positive thoughts pushed out many of those negative thoughts. Christ began a slow process of healing this broken man.

Healing and restoration can only come from faith and trust in Christ.

Through Christ, I slowly began the process of freeing myself from the chains that bound me. I built myself up—physically, spiritually, and mentally. I attacked my abandonment, rejection, trust, and self-esteem issues and placed my anger, fear, and worry in the Lord's hands. I began looking people in the eyes. I chose success, strength, courage, faith, and hope over despair, defeat, and lack.

Yes, that's right; it's a choice, one I willingly made.

I learned that the world isn't just filled with loss but instead wonderful opportunities. And, most importantly, that the Lord loves this Ohio orphan.

Now, don't get me wrong, folks. I still have problems, many, actually. I also sometimes resort back to negative, defeating thoughts. But I learned something very valuable—that faith and trust in Christ will eventually empower you with a spine of steel to conquer all obstacles. He will give you hope, new and better purposes, and change you for the better from the inside out.

After all, 2 Corinthians 5:17 states, "Therefore if anyone is in Christ, he is a new creature; the old things passed away; behold, new things have come." The Lord will perform wonders in your life if you just believe in him, invite him into your heart, and make him your Lord and Savior.

And long, long before my existence, the Lord performed miracles in other's lives too—ordinary people called to live extraordinary lives.

Just like me. Just like you.

People selected to suffer, all for the glory of the Lord.

Like Moses, a stutterer and murderer called to rescue the Lord's chosen people from bondage. Or Joseph, thrown into a pit by his brothers, sold to slavery, and then falsely accused and imprisoned, yet who eventually became prime minister of Egypt. And Job, a man relentlessly attacked by Satan.

But they, and we, all have one thing in common: the Lord. They succeeded even when their adversities, problems, and Goliaths seemed absolutely unbeatable. And so can you. For success is merely understanding and then fulfilling the Lord's purpose for your life.

With the Lord, anything is possible.

LONELINESS

I recall in my early forties lying in bed late one night feeling absolutely and totally alone. I was single, never married, the primary caregiver to my grandmother, and working a low-paying, dead-end job.

I felt that nobody cared about me, that I'd never fall in love, that I'd always be financially poor, and that I'd always just be a servant to others. Yep, a rip-roaring pity party, complete with party hats, confetti, and noisemakers. So much for practicing positive thinking, huh?

Thus, being a great man of faith, what did I do? The wrong thing. I griped and complained to Jesus.

"You have no idea whatsoever how lonely I am," I lamented. "When were you ever lonely? Do you even know what loneliness is?" Well, as is often the case, the Holy Spirit didn't put up with my ignorant ravings and replied right away to my inner being.

"Jim, put yourself in Jesus' position," the Holy Spirit said. "Nobody has ever been as lonely as Jesus. Think about it."

That got me a tad peeved, as I didn't feel like thinking about it but wanted to remain angry and pout. After a thumb sucking, I gave it some thought and hope you will too.

In John 1:14, it says, "And the Word became flesh, and dwelt among us, and we saw his glory, glory as of the only begotten from the Father, full of grace and truth." Yes, Jesus is Lord and Savior, but can you imagine his depths of loneliness here on earth? He was born in this world but isn't of this world. He had to live in this world with a bunch of filthy sinners (yep, like you and me, folks).

A king among ants.

A Cadillac among skateboards.

Infinite wisdom among more-than-limited capacities. Perfection among marred, flawed imperfection.

Besides his Father, with whom could he relate? Open up to? Share his hopes, concerns, worries, and fears?

For one moment of fantasy, imagine that *you* are Jesus as a teenager. (When Jesus was a teenager, I don't know if he had acne, a cracking, adolescent voice, and sprouts of sparse chin hairs, but let's look beyond that.)

What if you knew that come your early thirties, you would be severely beaten, flogged, have large, rusty nails pounded through both hands and feet and then hung for hours on a wooden cross, dying a slow and agonizingly incomprehensible death?

I'm sure you would sweat blood from fear just like Jesus did in the garden of Gethsemane if you had that to look forward to! You may even have some sleepless nights and more than a few panic attacks. I would.

So who would you turn to for comfort, reassurance, and strength? Your parents? Your best friend? A teacher or coach? Who could possibly understand such a dilemma and help you to prepare? Why, you'd either be laughed out of town or fitted for a straight jacket if you disclosed to others your impending crucifixion. And that's probably how Jesus felt. No one on earth could possibly begin to understand his situation.

Jesus understands loneliness more than anybody ever will. In fact, he understands anything and everything. Isaiah 40:28 says, "His understanding is inscrutable." Psalm 147:5 says, "Great is our Lord and abundant in strength; His understanding is infinite."

Infinite! Of course he understands and has compassion for my loneliness and yours too. Proverbs 2:6 says, "From his mouth come knowledge and understanding."

He's one all-knowing, all-understanding dude!

So if you are lonely, don't fret. You are not alone. Just crawl into your Father's lap and tell him all about it.

He's waiting.

STRESS

Stressed out. Tension laden. Heavily burdened.

Those unenviable words described me at age forty-five.

I lost my job as a newspaper reporter. I got laid off due to the economy. Then my ninety-six-year-old grandmother, who lived with me for ten years, broke her hip. Watching her in such pain burdened me greatly. She survived surgery and was placed in a nursing facility for rehabilitation. She died a few months later.

The stress from the never-ending medical bills, phone calls to and from medical personnel and the nursing home, Medicare/Medicaid/insurance paperwork, doctor's appointments, hospital/nursing home visits, etc., for my grandmother became overwhelming. I didn't have family near and had to handle all that responsibility on my own. That combined with not working and the loss of self esteem that results from that created quite a maelstrom for me.

I managed to keep my faith most of the time but

still, at times, resorted to worry and fear. All of the stress and worries also elevated my blood pressure to the prehypertension stage. Not good. I also had constant flulike symptoms as the result of anxiety.

Throughout the whole ordeal, I prayed and spoke with the Lord day and night. At times, I became angry with the Lord and let him know it. Fortunately, he doesn't get angry when I confront him. The great irony is that when I became angry and yelled at him due to my lack of understanding, that in itself was a powerful prayer because I acknowledged that he is my one and only hope. I didn't turn my back on him but instead poured my heart and soul to him, which he desires ever so much.

Psalm 103:8 says, "The Lord is compassionate and gracious, slow to anger and abounding in lovingkindness."

So how did I get through such a stressful time? I touched the Lord's robe, of course.

One of my favorite Bible stories concerns the woman with the issue of blood. The story tells of a woman who had a hemorrhage for twelve years. She couldn't stop bleeding. According to Luke 8:43, the woman "could not be healed by anyone." Talk about a stressful situation!

I think it's safe to assume that this woman went to many doctors and more than likely spent all her money on trying to stop the bleeding. Besides the huge financial toll, this woman also had to deal with the unyielding stress and anxiety caused by perpetual sickness.

One day, the woman heard that Jesus was coming to town. She knew that he was her last and only hope. She knew that if she could just touch Jesus or even just reach out and touch a teeny thread hanging on the bottom of his robe that she would be healed.

Now that's faith!

I'm sure that this woman was very weak and physically and emotionally exhausted. I can just picture this bent over, sweating, dust-covered, bleeding, pitiful creature stumbling across the dirt road to reach Jesus, possibly leaving a crimson trail.

Now understand that when Jesus visited towns, throngs and throngs of people surrounded him. Chaos, more than likely, with people reaching from all angles to touch Jesus, screaming and yelling at him to look their way, and wails and moans from those seeking healing and help.

Jostling. Shoving for position. Elbows flying and probably more than a few fists.

Undaunted, undeterred, and with fierce faith, this woman probably had to fight through the crowd to get to Jesus. She may have even needed to get on hands and knees to crawl between legs; some of which probably replied with a swift kick to her ribs. Crawling on all fours through animal excrement and who knows what else.

But she persevered and somehow, somehow managed to lunge, possibly with the last ounce of strength she possessed, and touched the fringe of his cloak.

Immediately, her bleeding stopped.

"Who is the one who touched me?" Jesus asked. That is one of the things I love about Jesus, when he played Columbo. Remember the Peter Falk television show, *Columbo*? Falk played a police detective who, at times, acted like he didn't know what he was doing. He purposely acted downright dumb sometimes. But we viewers knew that he was always the smartest person on the show.

I can picture Jesus playacting while looking confusedly about, trying to figure out who touched him in such a special way—first to the left, then the right, and for added effect, maybe even skyward. That, complete with helpless shrugs, scratching his head with his index finger, and sighs of exasperation.

For as the story goes, after the woman touched Jesus, healing electricity shot from his body and healed her instantly.

I assume Jesus knew who touched him and why. After a few moments of showing off his thespian skills, he then turned and placed his royal gaze on the woman.

She then needlessly explained why she did what she did.

"Daughter, your faith has made you well; go in peace," Jesus said (Luke 8:48).

This story is about you and me. No, I'm not a woman, but yes, I do have issues of blood, that is, problems, concerns, hurts, and fears. The point of the story is to show the miracles of healing that Jesus will provide if you just have faith and trust in him.

So what is bleeding in your life? Divorce? Sickness? Loneliness? Lack of finances? Like the woman with the issue of blood, your problems may have been going on for over a decade or even longer. But there is a cure. The Lord. He's waiting for you. He wants and greatly desires for you to come to him with your problems and concerns. He is your Father. He created you and knows everything about you.

He knows what you will think before you think it and knows what you will say before you speak it. However, he desires to have a relationship with you and wants you to verbally speak your concerns to him.

In Matthew, Jesus explains the cure for anxiety:

> For this reason I say to you, do not be worried about your life, as to what you will eat or what you will drink; nor for your body, as to what you will put on... Look at the birds of the air, that

they do not sow, nor reap nor gather into barns, and yet your heavenly Father feeds them. Are you not worth much more than they? And who of you by being worried can add a single hour to his life... So do not worry about tomorrow; for tomorrow will care for itself. Each day has enough trouble of its own.

Matthew 6:25–34

Do you want the blood to stop flowing in your life? Do you want to receive that same jolt of healing electricity that the woman with the issue of blood received? Do you want to be healed of your troubles or at least given the courage and strength to endure and cope?

Then it's quite simple, folks.

Just reach out and touch that robe.

FEAR

I've got one of those hearts that occasionally skips beats. It was initially alarming, but once I got used to the occasional skip, it became no big deal. However, one day, about nine years ago, my heart started skipping beats many times per minute all day long. Scared the living daylights out of me. As with most men, I didn't want to go to the doctor or the emergency room and hoped the problem would just disappear.

The thought of going to an emergency room scared me more the many heart skips, so I decided to just grin and bear it. Plus, I didn't have health insurance and didn't want to pay a giant hospital bill. I even went to the gym hoping a workout would calm my heart down. It didn't. Around midnight, I finally got scared enough to drag myself to the emergency room where they hooked me to a heart monitor.

I watched as the machine visually showed each time my heart skipped. The doctor then came into the room, looked at the machine, and expertly stated, "Yep, it's skipping all right." He then immediately left. I don't know what scared me more: that I thought I was dying or that I had an emergency room doctor who didn't seem to care.

After day-long heart tests days later, the doctor gave me a clean bill of health. He said, "You are fine. You just have one of those hearts that skips." That opened the door for many more questions from me, but he left before I could ask them.

This was obviously a man of few words and even fewer social skills.

While hooked up to that machine, fearful and scared, I recall repeating over and over, "Fear not, for I am with thee," as similarly stated in Genesis 26:24, Isaiah 43:5, and elsewhere. Repeating that nonstop while lying hooked to that heart monitor gave me a sense of peace, knowing that the Lord was there right beside me. Even though I was scared, I knew that I was in the Lord's very capable hands, as stated in Scripture.

That adventure reminded me of another favorite Bible story: when Jesus stills the wind and sea while in a boat. Beginning at Mark 4:35, Jesus decided to cross to the other side of the sea with his disciples. While in route, "there arose a fierce gale of wind, and the waves were breaking over the boat so much that the boat was already filling up. Jesus himself was in the stern, asleep on the cushion."

Now, I'm sure it's safe to assume that Jesus created that storm to see how his disciples would respond. Would they be fearful and afraid even though Jesus was right there with them? Or would they remain calm, trusting in Jesus to see them safely to the other side?

With whipping waves, thunder, lightning, and forceful, dangerous winds, those poor, soaked disciples must have been terrified. With the boat rocking about uncontrollably, they probably felt that they would be thrown into the foamy, angry sea to drown.

The disciples then woke Jesus and screamed, "Teacher, do you not care that we are perishing?"

Jesus then calmed the wind and said to the sea, "Hush, be still." It did. "Why are you afraid? How is it that you have no faith?" questioned Jesus.

This story shows that during our most frightening storms, Jesus is right there beside us. You may think that Jesus is asleep and not paying attention while you are being tossed and thrown about but not so. You may not sense it, feel it, or believe it, but he's there. Jesus not only calmed the wind and told the sea to "hush, be still," but in an indirect way, he made that command to his disciples too. He not only calmed the raging wind and sea, but he also calmed the raging wind and sea within his disciple's hearts. And he'll do that for you too during your most trying tests and trials.

He's, in essence, saying to us, "Hush, be still, my

child. I'm right here with you. You have absolutely nothing to fear. Absolutely nothing at all. I'm here, child, right here."

When hooked to a heart monitor with a heart that's beating like a boy banging on his toy drum, hush, be still.

When the bank calls and tells you that your home is in foreclosure, hush, be still.

When your child joins the armed forces and is sent overseas to fight terrorism, hush, be still.

When the biopsy states that you have breast cancer, hush, be still.

Proverbs 3:24–26 says, "When you lie down, you will not be afraid; When you lie down, your sleep will be sweet. Do not be afraid of sudden fear, nor of the onslaught of the wicked when it comes; For the Lord will be your confidence, and will keep your foot from being caught."

Notice how it says "the onslaught of the wicked when it comes." That may infer that evil by the devil will be sent your way at one time or another. Be prepared. Be ready. Equip yourself with Jesus.

Psalm 34:4 says, "I sought the Lord, and he answered me, and delivered me from all my fears." Seek the Lord. He will answer and calm your fears.

Deuteronomy 31:6 says, "Be strong and courageous, do not be afraid or tremble at them, for the Lord your

God is the one who goes with you. He will not fail you or forsake you."

And for any doubting Thomases still out there, guess what? According to Titus 1:2, it states that God cannot lie. He is so pure, holy, and righteous that no lie ever leaves his lips. Heed and believe his words, as they are truth, not lies. The devil is the master of lies while the Lord is the master of truth.

So why are you afraid? How is it that you have such little faith?

Hush, be still.

PATIENCE

I lose patience while being patient. The American Heritage College Dictionary defines patience as "bearing or enduring pain, difficulty, provocation, or annoyance with calmness." I must admit, at times, I lack patience. And I sometimes lose patience while trying to be patient.

I'm sure most people feel the same way. We want what we want when we want it. We hate to wait. Standing in line at the grocery store burns us up. Waiting for an unusually long red light burns us up. And yes, waiting for the Lord's promises to come to fruition burns us up.

I've often tried to pin the Lord down with a timetable. My own timetable, that is. Many times, I've tried to tell him when something good or important should happen in my life instead of waiting for his timing. Ever done that? "By age forty I'll have a wife and a house" or "By age forty-two I'll be debt-free; all my student loans and credit cards will be paid off" or "It's time to travel the nation to give my Christian testimony."

I recall years ago when I first started changing my thoughts from negative to positive. I started to believe in miracles and expected them. Really expected them. Sadly though, I went overboard. So much so that with every new phone call, every new e-mail, and every new postal delivery received, I expected miracles to arrive. When they didn't, I became angry and upset. This went on for years and led to deep frustration.

Yes, expect miracles. Yes, believe in miracles. They do happen but only in the Lord's timing. I eventually learned to have patience and wait for the Lord. I also learned that it's his will, not mine, that is important. I stopped putting a timetable on every aspect of my life and turned it over to the Lord. His will, not mine.

If he wants me to have something, he'll give it to me. Whatever he wants, he will provide just that. I just need to have patience and wait.

When speaking about patience, Abraham and Sarah come to mind. They wanted a son but were well advanced in age: Abraham, ninety-nine and Sarah, eighty-nine. Can you imagine having the patience to wait until their ages to have a son? Beginning with Genesis 18, the story says that the Lord appeared to Abraham through three men who promised him a son.

They said that they would return at the same time next year and that Sarah would have a son. Sarah was at the door listening and scoffed at such a notion, being well beyond child-bearing age. She also laughed.

"And the Lord said to Abraham, 'Why did Sarah laugh, saying, 'Shall I indeed bear a child, when I am so old?' Is anything too difficult for the Lord? At the appointed time I will return to you, at this time next year, and Sarah will have a son.'"

Thus, they had to be patient for yet another year! I'll bet each and every minute of each and every day just dragged and dragged while looking forward to that blessed event. They both might have even thought that they wouldn't even live another year, being of such advanced ages. I'm sure they both had doubts about whether to believe or not.

However, as the Lord promised, a year later, Sarah gave birth to a son.

Has the Lord ever laid something on your heart, but you scoffed and didn't believe? Has he ever told you that something spectacular would happen, a miracle, but you chose not to believe?

After being paralyzed, the Lord said that you would walk again, but you laughed and didn't believe?

After being single for half a century, the Lord said he would soon loan you the perfect mate, but you laughed and didn't believe?

You lost your job because of the economy, and the Lord said that you would go back to school to become a nurse, but you laughed and didn't believe?

Remember, the Lord can't lie. We must not only believe but also have patience too.

Second Timothy 4:2 tells us to have "great patience" while 1 Peter 2:20 says, "… But if when you do what is right and suffer for it you patiently endure it, this finds favor with God."

When dealing with patience, and everything else, Christ is our example.

> For you have been called for this purpose, since Christ also suffered for you, leaving you an example for you to follow in his steps, who committed no sin, nor was any deceit found in his mouth, and while being reviled, he did not revile in return; while suffering, he uttered no threats, but kept entrusting himself to him who judges righteously; and he Himself bore our sins in his body on the cross, so that we might die to sin and live to righteousness; for by his wounds you were healed. For you were continually straying like sheep, but now you have returned to the Shepherd and Guardian of your souls.
>
> 1 Peter 2:21–25

If the Lord said that he will do something, he will do it. He will make it happen. He can't lie. So be patient.

Is anything too difficult for the Lord?

OBEDIENCE

After I graduated from journalism school in the late 1990s, I got a job as a newspaper reporter near my hometown. I didn't have a place to stay and asked my grandmother if I could stay with her. She said yes.

While working that job, I searched for other places to live but soon realized I couldn't afford to live on my own with my meager paycheck. (You folks would be thoroughly shocked at the low pay in the newspaper journalism profession.) So I decided, out of necessity, to continue living with Granny. I hoped a better-paying position would eventually open up that would allow me to move and be independent.

Years went by, but the low pay and lack of other opportunities remained the same. Also, Granny's health began to decline. One day, when in her upper eighties, she experienced tremendous pain in her side. I took her to the hospital, which revealed a bad gallbladder. They removed it.

I began to realize that the Lord wanted me to be

with Granny. He wanted me to look out for her and to help her. However, I struggled with foolish, male pride, in that I felt that I shouldn't be living with my grandmother and should be out on my own.

Ah, yes, the I-should-be trap. A worthless and nonproductive phrase.

I should be married and have kids.

I should be making more money.

I should have my own home and a 401(k).

But guess what? It doesn't matter what I think I should have. It doesn't matter what I think that I want. What matters is the Lord's will for my life, as stated in the Lord's Prayer: "Thy will be done, on earth as it is in heaven" and also in Luke 22:42 when Jesus says before being crucified, "Father, if You are willing, remove this cup from Me; yet not My will, but Yours be done."

And as said in Romans 8:28: "And we know that God causes all things to work together for good to those who love God, to those who are called according to his purpose."

I began to see my situation in a different light. My grandmother took me in after the death of my parents, and now it was my turn to return the favor, to put my own selfish desires second and serve others, just like Jesus wants us to do.

To be obedient to his will. Just like Noah and Jonah.

Most are familiar with Noah. Beginning with Genesis 6, it says that the Lord saw the wickedness and violence of man and the evil thoughts in their hearts. He decided to do something about it. "I will blot out man whom I have created from the face of the land, from man to animals to creeping things and to birds of the sky; for I am sorry that I have made them" (Genesis 6:7). However, he favored Noah and his family members.

He told Noah to build the ark and fill it with animals, as he was going to destroy everything on earth with a flood. "Thus Noah did; according to all that God had commanded him, so he did" (Genesis 6:22).

Now put yourself in Noah's position. What if the Lord told you to build an ark to prepare for a great flood? Would you be obedient or ignore the Lord's commands? Can you imagine the comments, ridicule, and laughter from your neighbors and co-workers? I'm sure the media would get wind of it and write about your ark endeavor. David Letterman and other comedians would probably mock you, making you a national joke. If your town didn't already have a village idiot, they'd make you it.

I'm sure Noah faced such ridicule and scorn. Yet he never wavered with his faith and trust in God. He was obedient.

And what about Jonah? The story of Jonah demonstrates that we need to be obedient because we can run, but we can't hide from the Lord. Have you ever tried to run from what the Lord wanted you to do? I have. Have you ever tried to hide from the Lord? I have. Has the Lord ever sent a storm into your life to get your attention?

The story tells of Jonah, a prophet, chosen by the Lord to go to the city of Nineveh to preach a message of repentance. The Lord promised to destroy the city if the people didn't repent. Jonah refused and fled via a ship in the opposite direction.

Jonah didn't want to go preach to the people of Nineveh because he was afraid. They were a cruel and heartless people, barbarians, and Jonah feared for his very life.

According to Jonah 1:4, "The Lord hurled a great wind on the sea and there was a great storm on the sea so that the ship was about to break up." The crew soon learned that Jonah was the cause of the storm. Jonah implored them to throw him into the sea. "Pick me up and throw me into the sea. Then the sea will become calm for you, for I know that on account of me this great storm has come upon you" (Jonah 1:12).

The crew tossed Jonah, and the sea stopped raging. Then the Lord had a huge fish swallow Jonah. He spent three days and three nights in the fish's belly.

So let's get this straight. Instead of being obedient

to the Lord, Jonah would rather be hurled from a ship to drown? Then he doesn't pray to the Lord right away but stubbornly and brazenly waits a few days before asking to be released! Now, you know it wasn't the Ritz Carlton in that fish belly—horrible-smelling gastric juices, half-digested food, complete darkness, and who knows what else. He must have been beyond soaked and hungry.

Jonah became the epitome of stubbornness and bullheadedness, wouldn't you agree?

In Jonah 2:9, Jonah finally says, "But I will sacrifice to You with the voice of thanksgiving. That which I have vowed I will pay. Salvation is from the Lord."

The Lord heard and commanded the fish to vomit Jonah to land.

The Lord then commanded Jonah to once again go to Nineveh. And surprise, surprise, he did. The people of Nineveh repented, and the Lord spared the city.

Jonah initially thought he could hide from the Lord. But he couldn't, and neither can you or I. So it's best to be obedient to the Lord. Jeremiah 23:23–24 says, "Am I a God who is near, declares the Lord, and not a God far off? Can a man hide himself in hiding places so I do not see him… Do I not fill the heavens and the earth?"

This story also demonstrates that even when you run from the Lord, he will still pursue you. He loves you that much. He still loves you even when you are disobedient and will give you a second chance, a third chance, and beyond.

Romans 3:23-24 says, "For all have sinned and fall short of the glory of God, being justified as a gift by his grace through the redemption which is in Christ Jesus."

Are there areas in your life where you are being disobedient to the Lord? Are you in the fish's belly now? If so, pray for courage and strength that you'll be able to do what the Lord wants you to do.

Dry land awaits.

COURAGE

I heard of a study that said the number one fear people have is public speaking. People fear getting up in front of an audience and delivering a speech more than anything, even death. Jerry Seinfeld once joked that, according to that study, if at a funeral, most people would rather be in the casket than delivering the eulogy.

I must admit that I used to be afraid to give speeches. I recall years ago being honored by my alma mater, Bowling Green State University. I was excited, that is, until they said they wanted me to give a speech as part of the ceremony. I became afraid and nervous, as I'd be speaking in front of educated people—professors, staff, and students. I felt intimidated and rather unworthy of being the guest of honor.

I practiced my twenty-minute speech until I had it completely memorized. Come the day of my speech, I was very nervous but somehow managed to drag myself to the podium. At one moment, I felt a jolt of panic and felt like bolting. Wouldn't that have been a sight, seeing me sprinting out of the room and not stopping until I reached my car? However, I put my trust and faith in Jesus. I knew that he would give me the courage to do what I needed to do.

Joshua 1:9 says, "Be strong and courageous! Do not tremble or be dismayed, for the Lord your God is with you wherever you go." Repeating that gave me comfort and reassurance.

I delivered the speech and actually enjoyed it once I began speaking. I became less self-conscious, putting the emphasis on the speech, not myself.

Now, there is nothing wrong with being nervous before giving a speech. That's normal. I still get nervous before giving a speech, which is good. You want to be nervous because that shows that you care about your topic and want to do the very best job you can.

You can be afraid and courageous at the same time. Courage means that you have the strength that enables you to face your fears and be brave regardless of your fears. Before giving a speech, your knees may be knocking, your legs may feel like wet noodles, and you may be sweating as if you just walked under Niagara Falls, but shove that fear aside, grasp your God-given courage, and forge forward. You'll be surprised and proud of how well you'll do.

When speaking of courage, David comes to mind. Yes, David versus Goliath.

According to 1 Samuel, the Lord sent a prophet, Samuel, to Bethlehem to anoint a new king. He chose David, a shepherd and the youngest of Jesse's eight sons—an unlikely pick to human eyes but not to the Lord's.

"Do not look at his appearance or at the height of his stature, because I have rejected him; for God sees not as man sees, for man looks at the outward appearance, but the Lord looks at the heart," says 1 Samuel 16:7. Instead of choosing the older, stronger, and taller brothers, the Lord instructed Samuel to anoint David, a man he referred to in Acts 13:22 as "a man after my heart, who will do all My will."

People saw David as just a young shepherd boy, but the Lord saw a future king. He saw potential. He saw greatness.

Now it came about that an enemy, the Philistines, came to do battle with Israel. They brought a giant named Goliath, a nine-foot-plus wrecking machine who wore heavy armor and bore a javelin, sword, spear, and shield. The Israeli army was greatly afraid of Goliath. Besides his immense size and strength, he also possessed a big mouth, which he used to taunt, mock, and intimidate.

Goliath told King Saul's army to pick one of their men to come fight him. If that man could kill him, then the Philistines would become their servants. However, if he killed that man, then Israel and its people would become servants and serve the Philistines.

Knowing that the Lord was with him, David courageously volunteered. He approached the giant with just five stones and a sling.

When Goliath saw David approach, he became enraged and insulted that King Saul would send a youth to battle him. He cursed David and said, "Come to me, and I will give your flesh to the birds of the sky and the beasts of the field" (1 Samuel 17:44).

"I come to you in the name of the Lord of hosts, the God of the armies of Israel, whom you have taunted. This day the Lord will deliver you up into my hands, and I will strike you down and remove your head from you" (1 Samuel 17:45–46). Undaunted, David confidently and courageously prepared for battle.

For you see, Goliath was doomed from the beginning; he wore just the armor of man while David instead wore the armor of God.

Goliath then came to meet David, but David ran even quicker to meet Goliath. While running, David grabbed a stone from his pouch and slung it. Bonk! It hit Goliath's huge head right square in the forehead. He fell to the ground like a giant redwood tree just felled. David then took Goliath's sword and cut off Goliath's head. The Philistine army fled.

And so will your Goliaths if you have faith like David and wear the armor of god.

Psalm 27:14 says, "Wait for the Lord; Be strong and let your heart take courage; Yes, wait for the Lord." Psalm 31:24 says, "Be strong and let your heart take courage, all you who hope in the Lord."

And, "Be strong and courageous, do not fear or be dismayed … with us is the Lord our God to help us and to fight our battles," says 2 Chronicles 32:7–8.

There is a solution to conquering your Goliaths: pick up your stones of faith, your sling of truth, and your God-given courage. All Goliaths crumble and fall when confronted with the Lord's weapons.

FAITH

Faith is belief in the unseen, not the seen. It's not based on your temporary, earthly, circumstance but instead on the eternal salvation, grace, and love of the Lord.

> He who observes the day, observes it for the Lord, and he who eats, does so for the Lord, for he gives thanks to God; and he who eats not, for the Lord he does not eat, and gives thanks to God. For not one of us lives for himself, and not one dies for himself; for if we live, we live for the Lord, or if we die, we die for the Lord; therefore whether we live or die, we are the Lord's.
>
> Romans 14:6–8

My faith became stronger when I realized that the Lord created me for his, and only his, specific purposes. We are his creation, here to serve him and bring him glory. Bringing him glory can take time though.

I went back to college in my early thirties to earn a journalism degree. I hadn't yet become a born-again

Christian. I wanted to write for men's fitness magazines, those that incorporate professional health and fitness articles, but also utilize humor. I also wanted to write humor books. At that time, that was my passion, with emphasis on *my* passion. Doing that type of writing consumed me.

I spent years reading those types of magazines, trying to break into the business, and sending out many query letters to publishers and magazine editors. Although I did get published in a few magazines, nothing greater resulted.

As with lots of writers, I had a day job that paid working as a newspaper reporter. After spending lots of money to obtain my journalism degree, I became frustrated and dismayed that I wasn't hired to write for a fitness magazine. I knew that's what I wanted to do, but doors of opportunity were not being opened.

I wonder why.

Could it be that even though I had a great passion for that type of writing, the Lord had other plans for my life? That he had a different course he wanted me to travel? That he created me to do something else? Maybe some other type of writing or endeavor? Faith that the Lord had my life in his capable hands kept me going even though I didn't know what the heck was going on.

Then a funny thing happened. I remember sitting

in a chair in my bedroom when a thought came to mind: "I want to help America's orphans, help them have a better life by giving them college scholarships." From that moment on, my passion of wanting to write health and humor for fitness magazines and to write humor books completely vanished! The Lord replaced my passion with one of his. And better yet, he filled my being with more passion than I previously had via my other outlets. I learned that his will for my life is much greater and more rewarding than my own will for my life.

Then through faith and the Lord's favor, over the years, things began to evolve even further. The Lord kept adding other purposes he wants me to fulfill, such as saving souls by leading people to Christ.

If the Lord calls you, he will equip you with all the necessary ingredients to fulfill his purpose. It may be a bumpy and rough road to follow, but you need to have faith, perseverance, and patience. One thing I learned about the Lord is that he'll tell you to do things that you may think are impossible, things you may think you can't do.

Start my own business? How in the world can I do that?

Donate a kidney? How in the world can I do that?

Go to college? How in the world can I do that?

Alone, you can't. But with Christ you can. With him, anything is possible.

> Now faith is the assurance of things hoped for, the conviction of things not seen... By faith we understand that the worlds were prepared by the word of God, so that what is seen was not made out of things which are visible... And without faith it is impossible to please him, for he who comes to God must believe that he is and that he is a rewarder of those who seek him. By faith Noah, being warned by God about things not yet seen, in reverence prepared an ark for the salvation of his household... and became an heir of the righteousness which is according to faith.
>
> Hebrews 11:1–7

When speaking about faith, one individual from the Bible immediately comes to mind. This individual, a favorite of mine, not only demonstrated faith but tremendous, unbending, unrelenting faith. Though he suffered great trials and tribulations, he succeeded greatly due to the Lord's favor.

Joseph was the son of Jacob, later known as Israel. Beginning with Genesis 37:3, Jacob loved Joseph more than any of his other sons. This caused Joseph's brothers to hate him. Joseph was a dreamer, that is, he had dreams that foretold the future, and he could also interpret others' dreams. He had a dream as a youth that said he would reign over his brothers, which made his brothers hate him even more.

The brothers planned to kill Joseph but instead threw him into a pit. They then sold him into slavery to some traders who took him to Egypt. However, "the Lord was with Joseph, so he became a successful man" (Genesis 39:2). Joseph's master in Egypt saw how the Lord favored Joseph, and thus he made Joseph not only his personal servant but also put him in charge of everything he owned.

However, the wife of Joseph's master falsely accused Joseph of inappropriate behavior. Joseph was thrown in jail, but the Lord favored him, resulting in Joseph being put in charge of all the prisoners. Later, the king's cupbearer and baker offended the king and were sent to jail too.

The cupbearer and baker each had a dream. Joseph interpreted each; the cupbearer would be set free, and the baker would be hung. Both instances happened. Joseph asked the cupbearer, once released, to ask the king to release him from the dungeon. However, when set free, the cupbearer forgot about Joseph.

Two years later, Pharaoh, king of Egypt, had a dream and sent for Joseph for an interpretation. The dream told of seven years of abundance for Egypt followed by seven years of famine. Pharaoh then made Joseph prime minister of Egypt. During those seven years of abundance, Joseph stored grain in preparation for the famine.

During the famine, "the people of all the earth" came to Joseph to buy grain, including ten of Joseph's brothers. Joseph recognized his brothers, but they did not recognize him. Joseph tested his brothers and sent them away with grain.

Later, all of Joseph's brothers returned to Egypt to purchase more grain. Joseph tested them again and eventually revealed his true identity to them. Joseph forgave his brothers for what they did. "Now, therefore, it was not you who sent me here, but God; and he has made me a father to Pharaoh and lord of all his household and ruler over all the land of Egypt" (Genesis 45:8).

Joseph's entire family and descendants then moved to Egypt. They received the best of the land and prospered.

Hebrews 11:21–22 says, "By faith Jacob, as he was dying, blessed each of the sons of Joseph and worshiped, leaning on the top of his staff. By faith Joseph, when he was dying, made mention of the exodus of the sons of Israel, and gave orders concerning his bones."

What if your brothers hated you? What if you were thrown into a pit? What if you were sold into slavery? What if you were falsely accused and spent years in jail? What if you didn't deserve any of that but got it full measure?

Could you keep your faith and then forgive like Joseph?

This story demonstrates the power of the Lord's favor. Even when Joseph was being persecuted and mistreated, the Lord favored him and gave him courage, strength, and hope to endure.

And the Lord gives you his favor too.

If you have a job, you may not like it, but at least you have a job. If you have a home, you may not like it, but at least you have a home. Your clothing may be out-of-date, but at least you have clothing. Your shoes may be scuffed and old, but at least you have shoes. You may not like living on a budget, but at least you have food.

That's the Lord's favor. His grace is sufficient.

This story also demonstrates the power of forgiveness. You forgive people for their misdeeds against you because Christ forgives you for your sins. Since Christ forgives, we must forgive also. I doubt the Lord would have made Joseph prime minister of Egypt if he held a grudge against his brothers, however appropriate that grudge may seem to us. Joseph needed to display Christlike behavior to be elevated to the next level of leadership and responsibility.

Do you need to forgive someone? Are you harboring bitterness? If so, pray for Christ's help to relieve you of your burdens. He is faithful and will change your heart.

Great and unbelievable things can happen if you just have faith, not teeny-tiny faith but Grand-Canyon faith. The Lord created you to be "prime minister" of whatever his purpose is for your life.

Faith: it's only five letters but five letters that can miraculously change your life.

TRUST

Trust is difficult for me.

Due to early life experiences, I learned at an early age to be wary with trust. I thought that if you trust someone, he or she will eventually forsake you and leave you. Hurt you.

But I'm learning to trust, just like Paul.

> To keep me from exalting myself, there was given me a thorn in the flesh, a messenger of Satan to torment me—to keep me from exalting myself! Concerning this I implored the Lord three times that it might leave me. And he has said to me, "My grace is sufficient for you, for power is perfected in weakness." Most gladly, therefore, I will rather boast about my weaknesses, so that the power of Christ may dwell in me. Therefore I am well content with weaknesses, with insults, with distresses, with persecutions, with difficulties, for Christ's sake; for when I am weak, then I am strong.
>
> 2 Corinthians 12:7–10

It took me years to trust Jesus, but I've made great strides. I've learned that yes, the Lord truly is with me. I didn't used to believe it, as I didn't understand exactly what "the Lord is with me" meant.

"What does it matter if God is with me? I'm still broke."

"What does it matter if God is with me? I'm still single."

"What does it matter if God is with me, I'm still unhappy and sad."

But oh, it matters big time.

I recall two instances when I actually physically felt the Lord's presence. The first occurred when I lived in the mountains of North Carolina. My sister lived on top of a hill with a winding, curving, dirt driveway. My car had problems getting atop that hill, as I needed to drive as fast as possible; otherwise, I wouldn't make it up.

On one instance, while trying to get up that driveway, my brakes failed. I hadn't enough speed going up, and the car began to roll backward. I became concerned. Then more concerned. I knew that I was heading straight for a ravine off the driveway. I had no control over the car and tried to steer it toward a tree so that I wouldn't topple off the driveway. Then a funny thing happened.

A tingly, absolutely comforting, joyful feeling

engulfed my entire body. And I started laughing. Yes, laughing. All my fears vanished, replaced with calm comfort and assurance.

The presence of Jesus wrapped me in his arms.

The car, with ever-increasing speed, then hit a tree. The tree was flexible enough yet strong enough to bear the weight of the car and keep it from entering the ravine. I got out of the car, still feeling joyous, and saw that part of the car was dangling over the ravine. The tree was bent over, yet it held strongly. No damage resulted to the car.

I realized that the Lord was with me and that he purposely chose the right tree to hit. I got my brother-in-law to hop in the car and speed up the driveway for me. Even though the Lord was with me, I sure wasn't going to press my luck and get back in that car!

The second instance, once again, happened when in a car. (Maybe I should invest in a bicycle.) I was on a busy street when a car to the left unexpectedly zoomed out of a shopping plaza. Another car coming right toward me in the other lane veered to avoid it but struck it in such a way that the car coming toward me became airborne.

Yep, a ton-plus of menacing, airborne steel heading straight at me. So what happened?

You guessed it. That same wonderful, tingly, comforting feeling once again engulfed me. And yes, I laughed. Most wouldn't laugh when a car is airborne and about to smash into you. But when Jesus is with you, you have absolutely nothing to fear. Still tingling, I waited, completely without fear, for the inevitable, crushing impact.

Dink.

Somehow, while in the air and rushing toward me like Jaws, the car lost momentum and speed and just kissed my front fender. Just left a tiny mark too.

Do I now trust that the Lord is with me? Do I now know how important it is for the Lord to be with me? You betcha.

Joseph too was proof evident that the Lord gives favor and is with you, even during your most trying times. What if the Lord wasn't with Joseph and he didn't trust? Would he have been made head of his master's household? I doubt it. Would he have been made head over all the prisoners? I doubt it. Would he have been made prime minister of Egypt? I doubt it.

So while in unsavory situations, you want and need the Lord to be with you, as he will get you through those trying times with his favor and grace.

And secondly, "the Lord is with you" means that the Lord is working behind the scenes on your behalf. We don't know the Lord's future plans for us, but he does. We don't know what future blessings he has in store for us, but he does. That's why we need to trust him.

Your situation may make no sense whatsoever to you, but it makes complete sense to the Lord. That's all that matters.

Jeremiah 29:11 says, "For I know the plans that I have for you, declares the Lord, plans for welfare and not for calamity to give you a future and a hope."

Joseph sat in prison for years. He could have easily become distraught and given up on the Lord. But he was wise enough to realize that the Lord was working behind the scenes to give him "a future and a hope."

When I think of trust, I think of Abraham and Isaac.

Beginning with Genesis 22, God tested Abraham to check his trust and obedience. "Take now your son, your only son, whom you love, Isaac, and go to the land of Moriah, and offer him there as a burnt offering on one of the mountains of which I will tell you."

The Lord told Abraham to kill his son.

They arrived at their destination with wood for the burnt offering, fire, and a knife. Isaac questioned his father about where the lamb was for the offering. "God will provide for himself the lamb for the burnt offering, my son." They then came to the place God had selected.

Abraham built the altar and arranged the wood, bound Isaac, and placed him on the altar on top of the wood. Abraham then reared back with his knife to kill his son.

But the angel of the Lord called to Abraham and said, "Do not stretch out your hand against the lad, and do nothing to him; for now I know that you fear God, since you have not withheld your son, your only son, from Me" (Genesis 22:12). Abraham then lowered his knife and noticed a ram caught in the bushes. He took the ram and offered that as a burnt offering instead of Isaac.

The angel of the Lord again called to Abraham and said, "By Myself I have sworn, declares the Lord, because you have done this thing and have not withheld your son, your only son, indeed I will greatly bless you" (Genesis 22:16–17).

Can you begin to imagine the trust in the Lord possessed by Abraham? He trusted and obeyed the Lord to such an extent that he willingly was going to kill his son. If that's what the Lord wanted, for him to slay his son, then he would be obedient. He truly thought that his son would die by his hand. He had no idea that the Lord would stop him right before the slaying.

Killing his son would have completely devastated Abraham, but he trusted and loved the Lord enough to do the Lord's will.

Do you trust like Abraham?

Obey the Lord, and he will greatly bless you too.

LOSS

Since you've read about my life's losses, I'll go straight to a biblical example. When thinking of someone who was selected to suffer, Job comes to mind.

The story of Job tells of Job, a righteous man in the Lord's eyes, a very important and wealthy man. Job 1:1 says that Job was "blameless, upright, fearing God and turning away from evil."

In the story, God agrees to allow Satan to destroy Job's life. Satan hopes that in doing so that Job will crumble and curse the Lord. In Job 1:12, the Lord says, "Behold, all that he has is in your power, only do not put forth your hand on him." Thus, the Lord allowed Satan to test Job.

Things got real bad for Job, beginning with Job 13. His oxen and donkeys were stolen, and some of his servants were murdered. Then his sheep and some other servants were destroyed, his camels stolen, and his sons and daughters died.

After hearing of all the tragedies, Job didn't curse

the Lord, blame him, or sin. "Naked I came from my mother's womb, and naked I shall return there. The Lord gave and the Lord has taken away. Blessed be the name of the Lord."

Could you have shown such loyalty?

Satan again presented himself before the Lord and asked the Lord to allow him to once again attack Job. The Lord agreed. Satan "smote Job with sore boils from the sole of his foot to the crown of his head" (Job 2:7). Yet even though Job's "pain was very great," he didn't curse the Lord or sin. In Job 2:10, Job asked, "Shall we indeed accept good from God and not accept adversity?" However, he did wish he were never born and greatly lamented his situation.

With his friends, Job then searched for answers to his suffering. However, his friends weren't much help. Sometimes they offered good advice and sometimes bad advice.

One friend said that the innocent do not suffer, inferring that Job deserved his situation.

Job continued to suffer and became more and more discouraged, as shown beginning with Job 7. "Therefore I will not restrain my mouth; I will speak in the anguish of my spirit, I will complain in the bitterness of my soul... So that my soul would choose suffocation, death rather than my pains."

Another friend then told Job that God rewards the good and those with integrity.

In Job 10, Job replied, "I loathe my own life; I will give full vent to my complaint; I will speak in the bitterness of my soul." He also questioned the Lord. "Your hands fashioned and made me altogether, and would You destroy me? Why then have You brought me out of the womb? Would that I had died and no eye had seen me!"

Job's third friend rebuked Job and continued that Job deserved his fate.

Besides being angry with the Lord, Job also burned anger toward his friends. In Job 12, he said, "But I have intelligence as well as you; I am not inferior to you...Who among all these does not know that the hand of the Lord has done this? He later accused his friends of being "sorry comforters."

In Job 17:1, Job felt insulted and continued his downward spiral. "My spirit is broken, my days are extinguished, the grave is ready for me."

Poor Job. He desperately needed comfort and answers to his suffering but got verbally attacked by his friends, who felt that Job was unjust in the Lord's eyes. However, Job maintained his faith and trust in God and affirmed his righteousness and integrity in the Lord's eyes.

Eventually God answered Job, beginning with Job 38, by showing his mighty power

"Where were you when I laid the foundation of the

earth? Tell Me, if you have understanding...Have you ever in your life commanded the morning, and caused the dawn to know its place...Have you understood the expanse of the earth? Tell Me, if you know all this."

In Job 40:4, Job replied, "Behold, I am insignificant; what can I reply to You? I lay my hand on my mouth."

The Lord continued to tell Job of his power and might.

Job humbles himself, beginning with Job 42. "I know that You can do all things, and that no purpose of Yours can be thwarted...Therefore I have declared that which I did not understand...Therefore I retract, and I repent in dust and ashes."

The Lord was pleased with Job's response. He then rebuked Job's friends, as he felt that they didn't speak of "what is right as My servant Job has."

Job never sinned or cursed the Lord during his most trying and horrifying times. Job was also wise enough to repent and understand that the Lord is Lord, and we, as puny humans, can't begin to comprehend his wisdom and mightiness but must accept his will. Contrary to what his friends said, Job remained righteous throughout his whole ordeal.

Job passed the test.

According to Job 42:10, the Lord restored Job's fortunes. "The Lord restored the fortunes of Job when he prayed for his friends, and the Lord increased all that

Job had twofold...The Lord blessed the latter days of Job more than his beginning."

Even though Job's friends weren't much support at times, which greatly angered Job, Job forgave them and sincerely prayed for them. We learn from Job that we need to worship the Lord in whatever situation we are in whether good or bad. Job worshipped the Lord when things were going great and also when going quite badly.

Job's animals were stolen and destroyed. Yet he blessed the Lord.

Some of Job's servants were murdered. Yet he blessed the Lord.

Job's sons and daughters died. Yet he blessed the Lord.

Job's entire body festered with painful boils. Yet he blessed the Lord.

Don't be those types of Christians who are all sunshine and light when things go well, but once things take a nasty turn, they stop worshiping the Lord. They only give thanks when they are happy and their circumstances are grand. Nope. Be like Job and worship the Lord in all circumstances, good and bad.

Psalm 34:17–18 says, "The righteous cry, and the Lord hears and delivers them out of all their troubles. The Lord is near to the brokenhearted and saves those who are crushed in spirit."

Yes, Job reached a point of despair that he no longer wanted to live. The losses were too great. The pain was too great. He also questioned the Lord as to his actions and why the Lord would allow such things to happen to him. Job was only human and just wanted answers. However, even though he questioned the Lord and wished he had never been born, he remained loyal to the Lord and pure in his eyes.

Like Job said, "Shall we indeed accept good from God and not accept adversity?" Whether in abundance or in a pit, be like Job and praise the Lord at all times.

IMPORTANCE OF TITHING

Are you in debt? Do you live paycheck to paycheck? Do you never seem to have enough money to buy basics and necessities, not to mention the occasional luxury? If so, a five-letter word can change your life.

Tithe.

I was never a big church tither. As a matter of fact, I rarely gave money to my church because I instead gave to charity. I thought that giving to charity was the same as giving to the church. However, I learned that you need to first give a tithe, 10 percent of your income, to the church and that anything more than that is called an offering.

My church held an experiment, an experiment of testing and trust. It was called the Ninety-day Tithing Challenge. It was based on the book of Malachi that says God commanded a tithe, that if you don't tithe, you are robbing God, and that he wants us to test his faithfulness.

> Will a man rob God? Yet you are robbing Me!

But you say, "How have we robbed You?" In tithes and offerings. You are cursed with a curse, for you are robbing Me, the whole nation of you! "Bring the whole tithe into the storehouse, so that there may be food in My house, and test Me now in this," says the Lord of hosts, "if I will not open for you the windows of heaven and pour out for you a blessing until it overflows. Then I will rebuke the devourer for you, so that it will not destroy the fruits of the ground; nor will your vine in the field cast its grapes," says the Lord of hosts. "All the nations will call you blessed, for you shall be a delightful land," says the Lord of hosts.

Malachi 3:8–12

The people of Israel were being unfaithful to God with their giving, and the Lord pointed that fact out to them. Rather clearly, wouldn't you say?

Leviticus 27:30–32 says, "Thus all the tithe of the land, of the seed of the land or of the fruit of the tree, is the Lord's; it is holy to the Lord ... For every tenth part of herd or flock, whatever passes under the rod, the tenth one shall be holy to the Lord."

The Lord considered a tithe as his, and if not given, he considered it stealing from him. In other words, the Lord owns everything. Anything you can think of, he owns. It's all his. He allows us to keep 90 percent of what we earn but wants us to give 10 percent back.

The Ninety-day Tithing Challenge had two parts to choose from: either you already tithe, have seen God's faithfulness, and will continue to tithe, or secondly, you will take the challenge for ninety days by tithing ten percent of your income. If after ninety days you weren't convinced of God's faithfulness to bless you, then a full refund would be given.

I decided to take the challenge, signed the official form, and, as stated in Malachi, tested the Lord.

I believed and trusted that due to the challenge, something good would happen in my life. I wasn't sure if a miracle would happen in the ninety-day period but believed that tithing was the only way to make a miracle happen. I continued to tithe 10 percent to the church for ninety days.

Then something happened.

Just twelve days after I completed the Ninety-day Tithing Challenge, I was offered a professional book contract. I was told others in the church also received various blessings by taking part in the tithing challenge. Guess what? I now tithe weekly. I tithe because I don't want to steal from the Lord and also because I want to be blessed.

However, you may still not be convinced in the power of the tithe. You may think that you needn't pay attention to an order from the Old Testament. Yes, the Lord commanded the tithe in the Old Testament, but when Jesus came along, he put a new twist on it.

Matthew 23:23 says, "Woe to you, scribes and Pharisees, hypocrites! For you tithe mint and dill and cummin, and have neglected the weightier provisions of the law: justice and mercy and faithfulness; but these are the things you should have done without neglecting the others." Jesus said that it is good to tithe but that you also need to have justice, mercy, and faithfulness, that is, a relationship with him.

Yes, I'll certainly continue to tithe and not just because I want miracles to happen. When you tithe, it is a powerful way of saying that the Lord comes first in your life. He is the only thing that matters. He is the only one who can save your soul, bless you, and perform miracles in your life.

When you tithe to the church, you are in essence not giving to the church but instead to God. That shows that he comes first. You pay him before you do anything else. That demonstrates your love and devotion to him. It shows that you desperately want a relationship with him. He's number one in your life.

You may feel that you don't have enough money to tithe. You may feel that you are in so much debt that there is no earthly way that you can tithe. That's exactly why you need to tithe! When you tithe, the Lord's spirit takes over and protects and provides. That's where trust and faith come into play. When you tithe, you will find that somehow, somehow you have enough money to pay your bills. You can somehow live off of 90 percent (after you tithe) better than you did when keeping 100 percent of your income.

When you tithe, miracles happen. Some might be big, some might be small, but miracles nonetheless. Jesus will provide.

He may give you a pay raise at work.

He may give you an unexpected check.

He may keep you from getting sick.

He may keep your car from breaking down.

He may let your favorite college football team win the national title.

He may introduce you to your future wife or husband.

Besides being awarded a book contract, the Lord provided in other ways too. Although laid off, the Lord provided enough money in my savings account to be able to stay home and write. He also provided a quality laptop computer, a gift from my uncle, so that instead of using the library's computers, I could sit in my quiet apartment and write undisturbed. The Lord also provided food, clothing, shelter, and other blessings.

When you tithe, miracles happen. Do you want miracles to happen in your life? You can't afford not to tithe. Show the Lord that he is number one in your life.

Test him on it.

DARE

One of my all-time favorite quotes came from Norman Vincent Peale: "Dare to be what your best self knows you ought to be. Dare to be a bigger human being than you have ever been. Have great hopes, and dare to go all out for them. Have great dreams and dare to live them. Have tremendous expectations, and believe in them."

To dare simply means to have the courage to do something that requires boldness. You dare when you step out of your comfort zone to try something new. Could be anything. Are you stepping out in faith and daring to be great? What does the Lord want you to dare to do?

Go back to school to become a teacher or nurse?

Become a missionary and travel to another part of the world?

Adopt a child?

Run for city council?

One daring thing that I recall doing was going back

to school as a nontraditional student. I was in my thirties and working as a bartender in the mountains of North Carolina. It wasn't fulfilling work for me, and I knew I didn't want to do that for the rest of my life. I liked to write, so I decided to go to journalism school. Plus, it was in my blood, as my father was a newspaper editor and columnist at a major newspaper.

So I quit my job and moved back to Ohio. I took some journalism courses at the local community college to make sure that I liked journalism. I did, so I applied for journalism school at my alma mater, Bowling Green State University.

A few years later, after being accepted, I crammed all my belongings into my little Honda and headed for Bowling Green. I stayed a couple of weeks at my aunt's home until I found an apartment off campus. Once I did, I took summer classes. I recall freaking out because with college summer courses, you received the same number of credits as if it were a semester course, but they crammed a semester's worth of work into several weeks. I had hours and hours of homework each day and oftentimes wondered what in the heck I got myself into.

Some courses were very difficult for me, those that implemented computer work, like Photo Shop and QuarkXPress. I had never seen or heard of those computer programs before. I had very little computer knowledge and also never had e-mail until attending journalism school. I recall having to create and design a magazine cover via the computer. Most of the students, much younger than I, had no problems with such an assignment, as they were brought up with computers. They also knew those computer programs from other classes. I felt inferior, and I must admit, rather dumb at times, but I dared to not give up.

I had more than a few panic attacks due to being introduced to all that new technology, which I found intimidating. I had to first learn the basics of a computer. I didn't even know what that little trashcan was on the screen, how to use a floppy disk, or even how to turn on a computer. If that weren't enough, I had to learn complicated (to me) computer programs, all within weeks! Plus, I was getting graded on my work, which added to the pressure.

Thanks to the Lord, I dared to keep trying, I dared to endure, and I dared not to quit. I gave it my very best. I met with the professor many times after hours seeking help and assistance. Fortunately, I received a passing grade in that class but only because the professor realized that I gave great effort, not because of my computer savvy.

When thinking of a biblical character who dared to be great, Moses comes to mind. Yes, he had flaws and insecurities, but the Lord still used him in a tremendous way.

Beginning with Exodus 2, Moses was the son of

Hebrew slaves but was raised by Pharaoh's daughter. When grown, he killed an Egyptian who was beating one of his brethren. Moses then fled to another land. Later, an angel of the Lord appeared to him via a burning bush. The Lord then spoke to Moses, telling Moses that he had heard the cries of his chosen people and would rescue them from bondage from the Egyptians. But that he would use Moses to accomplish that goal.

Moses, however, didn't feel that he could handle such a monumental task.

Exodus 3:11 says, "But Moses said to God, 'Who am I, that I should go to Pharaoh, and that I should bring the sons of Israel out of Egypt?'" God told Moses that "certainly I will be with you."

Moses felt that he was unworthy and not capable. He felt that someone else would do a much better job than he. Have you ever felt that way? I have.

> Then Moses said to the Lord, "Please, Lord, I have never been eloquent, neither recently nor in time past, nor since You have spoken to Your servant; for I am slow of speech and slow of tongue." The Lord said to him, "Who has made man's mouth? Or who makes him mute or deaf, or seeing or blind? Is it not I, the Lord? Now then go, and I, even I, will be with your mouth, and teach you what you are to say."
>
> Exodus 4:10–12

Moses once again tried to talk the Lord out of his wishes. Moses' lack of confidence and mounting fear became apparent. I'm not certain exactly what burdened Moses with his speaking ability, whether he stuttered or had some other speech disability. However, it was enough to make Moses feel inferior and lacking.

Exodus 4:14 says that "the anger of the Lord burned against Moses."

Could that mean that the Lord became angry due to the doubts of Moses? Because Moses tried to talk his way out of serving the Lord? Or because the Lord felt that Moses didn't trust him enough to realize that the Lord would be with him and help him succeed?

Then, believe it or not, in Exodus 6:12 and Exodus 6:30, Moses again has doubts and told the Lord that he was "unskilled in speech."

Newsflash, Moses. The Lord knows you have a speech impediment. He knows all about you. He created you. He made you with his own hands. He knows absolutely everything about you. So stop selling yourself short. The Lord picked and chose you and anointed you for success.

Put yourself in Moses' position. The Lord wanted Moses to go speak to Pharaoh, the king of Egypt, but Moses was afraid. He obviously was very self-conscience about his speech difficulties. Why would the

Lord choose someone with a speech impediment to go speak to the king?

It may be that the Lord chooses humble people, those who realize their shortcomings and are not prideful and arrogant. It may be that the Lord chooses people who are average and ordinary to do his bidding. It may be that the Lord makes us confront our weaknesses, makes us painfully aware of them, and then helps us to overcome them. It may be that the Lord was not only saving his people from bondage but also saving Moses from bondage—his own lack of confidence and self-assuredness.

Could it be that the Lord wants us to realize that we are nothing without him? That when we are at our weakest that is when the Lord's power is made perfect? That he wants us to trust him 100 percent, even when he asks us to do something that we greatly fear and are insecure about?

Although probably trembling with fear and doubts, what did Moses do? He dared. He dared to be great. He dared to take the Lord's word as truth. He dared to step out of his comfort zone and to serve the Lord. He dared to speak to the king many times.

Pharaoh finally let God's people go, but Moses still had hardships to face.

However, Pharaoh had a change of heart and decided he didn't want to free the slaves after all. He chased after them with "six hundred select chariots, and all the other chariots of Egypt with officers over all of them" (Exodus 14:7). The children of Israel became very frightened when they saw the approaching army on their heels.

Exodus 14:13–14 says, "But Moses said to the people, 'Do not fear! Stand by and see the salvation of the Lord which he will accomplish for you today; for the Egyptians whom you have seen today, you will never see them again forever. The Lord will fight for you while you keep silent.'"

Moses then parted the Red Sea, which eventually engulfed the Egyptian army that was chasing the children of Israel.

It took great daring for Moses to lead the people from bondage and to lead them into a new land. Even though Moses had tremendous faith, I'm sure that he was quite nervous under such traumatic and stressful circumstances. Who wouldn't be? However, he dared to believe and trust the Lord and thus came out on top.

And you can too. The Lord still performs miracles. He still calls ordinary people to do extraordinary things. You may stutter. You may be shy. You may not think that you are attractive enough or smart enough. You may feel that you have no talents whatsoever.

Well, guess what? You are exactly whom the Lord

wants to use. The Lord doesn't look for perfect people to further his causes. If he did, he wouldn't find any. None.

So dare to be great. Dare to step out of your comfort zone. Dare to hope, to dream, and to believe.

I dare you.

POWER OF PRAYER

In a letter of Paul to the Colossians, Paul gives a list of rules for a Christ-centered life. In Colossians 4:2–3, it says "Devote yourselves to prayer, keeping alert in it with an attitude of thanksgiving; praying at the same time for us as well, that God will open up to us a door for the word, so that we may speak forth the mystery of Christ."

Over the years, I've learned to devote myself to prayer. I'm not yet at the devoted and anointed stage that Paul was, but I'm growing in my faith all the time. Prayer helps me get closer to the Lord and deepens my faith and trust. The Lord wants you to pray because he wants a relationship with you. He wants you to come to him with your problems, concerns, hopes, dreams, goals, and all the little details of your life. Nothing is too small or insignificant to him.

Don't be intimidated by prayer. Prayer is just talking to Jesus, the most compassionate, loving, and kind father you'll ever encounter. He will never laugh at you or mock you but instead give his undivided attention to your prayers.

And forget using what you think are big, holy, righteous words. Believe me; he's not impressed. He's much more impressed when you come to him and just talk and open your heart and soul to him the best way that you can. Nothing grandiose, pompous, and pretentious but instead heartfelt, true, humble, and honest.

> When you pray, you are not to be like the hypocrites; for they love to stand and pray in the synagogues and on the street corners so that they may be seen by men. Truly I say to you, they have their reward in full. But you, when you pray, go into your inner room, close your door and pray to your Father who is in secret, and your Father who sees what is done in secret will reward you. And when you are praying, do not use meaningless repetition as the Gentiles do, for they suppose that they will be heard for their many words. So do not be like them; for your Father knows what you need before you ask him.
>
> Matthew 6:5–8

He wants you to not only pray for others but to also pray for yourself. Christians sometimes feel that they shouldn't pray for themselves. They sometimes feel that they should only devote themselves to the welfare of others. That's true in a sense, in that we are servants of Jesus Christ, but you also need to pray for yourself. After all, you may be the only one praying for you! Everybody needs to have someone praying for him or her, so cover your bases and pray for yourself. Again, the Lord wants you to come to him with your entire being. Talk to him.

> Ask, and it will be given to you; seek, and you will find; knock, and it will be opened to you. For everyone who asks receives, and he who seeks finds, and to him who knocks it will be opened. Or what man is there among you who, when his son asks for a loaf, will give him a stone? Or if he asks for a fish, he will not give him a snake, will he? If you then, being evil, know how to give good gifts to your children, how much more will your Father who is in heaven give what is good to those who ask him!
>
> Matthew 7:7–11

Through prayer, I've gotten to know the Lord better, which has great benefits. Prayer calms me and fills me with a sense of warmth and comfort. It fills me with joy, at times, because I not only feel the presence of the Holy Spirit, but I also know that I'm helping both myself and others. It also demonstrates that I know that I'm nothing without the Lord and that he is my only hope and salvation.

The Bible says to pray unceasingly. That doesn't mean that you continuously pray, that you literally pray nonstop for twenty-four hours a day. All it means is that throughout the day, you talk to Jesus.

Jesus, I was just diagnosed with cancer. Please give me courage and strength.

Jesus, I just lost my job. Please find me another.

Jesus, I'm worried about my future. Please give me hope.

Jesus, I'm late for work. Please lessen traffic for me.

Jesus, please let the Ohio State Buckeyes win another national college football title soon.

If you earnestly ask Jesus for something, that then becomes a prayer. That something could be anything. No prayer that you sincerely seek is too trivial for the Lord. The Bible says that Jesus hears all your prayers. He doesn't always answer prayers, but he does hear and consider them all. Even just casual talk with Jesus throughout the day is a form of prayer, as you recognize and know that Jesus is real and your only hope and salvation.

Lately, when I wake in the morning, I give a quick prayer. I do this whether I feel well or not. I pray during both the good times and bad. I first say aloud Psalm 118:24: "This is the day which the Lord has made; Let us rejoice and be glad in it." Next, I say, "Jesus, thank you for your favor. Thank you for your grace. Thank you for your blessings. Please give me the courage and strength to do what I need to do today." I say that and mean that.

I then say the prayer of Jabez, at 1 Chronicles 4:10, that says: "Oh that You would bless me indeed and enlarge my border, and that Your hand might be with me, and that You would keep me from harm that it may not pain me!" The next sentence says, "And God granted him what he requested."

I love that prayer because Jabez specifically asks the Lord to bless him and only him. He says me four times with passion, fervor, and expectation. And the Lord responded. Jabez knew that there was only one God and that God was the only one who can bless him. Jabez knew his only hope was to seek out the Lord and put his faith and trust in him.

He asked to be greatly blessed and received it.

He asked to have his sphere of influence increased and received it.

He asked that the Lord would be with him and received it.

He asked to be kept from harm and pain and received it.

First Chronicles 5:20 says, "For they cried out to God

in the battle, and he answered their prayers because they trusted in him."

The Lord won't grant every prayer that you ask, but he does hear every word. He will take everything you say into consideration. He'll decide what you need and what he wants you to have. But, as proven in Scripture time and time again, the Lord does and will grant prayers. So ask away!

Jeremiah 29:12–13 says, "Then you will call upon Me and come and pray to Me, and I will listen to you. You will seek Me and find Me when you search for Me with all your heart."

Prayer is a great way to start the day right when you wake up. It sets the tone of the day and reinforces that the Lord comes first in your life.

Then throughout the day, I talk to Jesus while in the car, while in the gym, while in the store, etc. It's sort of an ongoing conversation with the Lord, as if he were right next to me, which he is. It can be about the weather, about what I'm going to have for dinner, or about anything. Talking to him is a form of prayer because you are acknowledging that you believe in him and that he is number one in your life. I also repeat memorized Bible verses.

I also like to shoot quick, heartfelt prayers at people I encounter or learn of throughout the day—people I don't know, people that I feel need a prayer, people that need compassion and empathy.

"Jesus, please give that woman I saw in that wheelchair courage, strength, and hope."

"Jesus, please help and heal those little girls I saw on the evening news. Their father just died in a boat accident."

"Jesus, that elderly woman across the street just broke her ankle. Please help her to get around."

"Jesus, please lessen the pain of that grocery store cashier who has carpal tunnel syndrome."

"Jesus, I'm at the gym now, and I want you to bless every person in this building. Please help them to reach their fitness goals."

I even pray in the middle of the night when I wake up and can't get back to sleep. But in this instance, I repeat Bible verses until I fall back asleep. My favorites are Proverbs 3, Psalm 23, and the Lord's Prayer. I'll also, on occasion, play the alphabet game. I'll start with the letter A, trying to think of a Bible verse that begins with that letter. Once accomplished, I move to letter B, and so on. I usually fall asleep before I reach the end of the alphabet.

I'm mentioning my prayer life to give you prayer ideas. Try these or incorporate your own prayer habits. All that matters is that you pray and talk to Jesus. If prayer is new to you, pick some of your favorite verses from the Bible and memorize them. Repeat them throughout the day. You'll find that they will give you strength and hope.

Prayers for others and yourself hold great power. James 5:16 says, "The effective prayer of a righteous man can accomplish much."

And of course, when you pray, pray with thanksgiving. Continuously thank the Lord for his many blessings, for the ones you see and for those unseen. Thank him and then thank him again. You may be going through some terrible times, but he will give you courage, strength, and hope to endure. Just pray and ask.

Rejoice. If Jesus is your Lord and Savior, when you die, you are going to heaven to spend eternity with him in paradise!

> First of all, then, I urge that entreaties and prayers, petitions and thanksgivings, be made on behalf of all men, for kings and all who are in authority, so that we may lead a tranquil and quiet life in all godliness and dignity. This is good and acceptable in the sight of God our Savior, who desires all men to be saved and to come to the knowledge of the truth. For there is one God, and one mediator also between God and men, the man Christ Jesus, who gave himself as a ransom for all, the testimony given at the proper time. For this I was appointed a preacher and an apostle (I am tell-

ing the truth, I am not lying) as a teacher of the Gentiles in faith and truth. Therefore I want the men in every place to pray, lifting up holy hands, without wrath and dissension.

1 Timothy 2:1–8

And lastly, I pray, "Jesus, I'm a sinner. I've said, thought, and done many a bad thing throughout my life. I'm trying to be the best person I can, so please have patience with me and help me to be what you want me to be. I'm nothing without you. I just have one thing more to say. Thank you."

IMPORTANCE OF TIMING

Timing, like patience, is difficult for me. Waiting for timing takes time because the timing I wait for comes in the Lord's time, not mine.

Being in tune with what and when the Lord wants me to do something is oftentimes hard to discern. Have you ever done something that you thought the Lord wanted you to do, but it didn't seem to work out? However, months, or years down the road, it finally did? That the Lord took you down various confusing paths that eventually led to where he wanted you to be?

An example from my life happened when I was working as a newspaper reporter. I had become bored and disenchanted with my job. I did a professional job, yet the pay was terrible and the workload heavy. I wanted to serve the Lord in a better way and felt that the Lord wanted me to go in a different direction. So I quit my job to instead give my Christian testimony to churches and various groups. I had no offers, only a tugging to go in that direction. I hoped to make that my livelihood.

Things didn't work out as I planned, though. Not many opportunities opened up, and I began to wonder if I had understood the Lord correctly or whether I had made a big mistake in quitting my job. After months of effort, nothing major happened. I then began to sense the Lord telling me that the timing for that particular endeavor wasn't right.

However, not wanting to go back into the newspaper business, months later, I reluctantly took another job at a local community newspaper. It was something I knew how to do, and due to the economy, there weren't any great job openings around anyway. I wasn't sure why the Lord wanted me to go back into journalism but figured he wanted me to keep writing.

After approximately ten months, I got laid off. Getting laid off is very stressful. As the economy continued to worsen, I became more and more anxious. As would most, I wondered how I'd pay my bills and what would happen to me. For the most part, I held onto my faith and trusted that the Lord would take care of me. He always has, so there was no reason to think otherwise.

Sometimes getting laid off is the best thing that can happen to you. It can make you reevaluate your life, assess your strengths and weaknesses, help to make you figure out what your God-given purpose really is, and get you closer to the Lord.

After months of feeling sorry for myself and trying to figure out what the Lord wanted me to do, I got a big urge to write a Christian book. It was the perfect opportunity and one I dared to take. Once again, I felt that the Lord was calling me in a certain direction. Of course, I had some doubts, as I didn't know whether I had the courage and strength for another intense endeavor. And if I failed, I certainly didn't want to face another major disappointment. I also worried that this, once again, may be my idea, and not the Lord's. Regardless, I forged ahead with renewed enthusiasm and hope, trusting in the Lord.

Sensing and acting on the Lord's timing takes time, patience, and understanding.

I put together a book proposal, sample chapters, etc., and sent it to a Christian book publisher. That publisher rejected it. I then prayed to the Lord to lead me to the book publisher that he wanted. I prayed that the Lord would choose one for me if that was his will. On my second try, my book proposal was accepted.

I now understand that things happened in the Lord's perfect timing; he wanted me to work those newspaper jobs so that I'd keep honing my skills, he led me to a job where he knew I'd get laid off, and then he provided the perfect time, opportunity, and resources for such an endeavor.

As I write this book, I'm not certain what will result

from it. I don't know what plans the Lord has in store for me. For the most part, I've quit trying to figure out what the Lord will do next and what the future holds. But I've learned that no matter how winding and crazy my path may seem, the Lord is in complete control. My path isn't crazy to him at all, as his paths are always perfectly laid.

And looking back on my life, all the craziness, all the tests and trials, all the confusion, were perfectly orchestrated by the Lord. Perfectly orchestrated, like a symphony, to eventually bring beautiful music and glory to him.

When thinking of timing, Ecclesiastes immediately comes to mind. There is a set time for everything.

> There is an appointed time for everything. And there is a time for every event under heaven—A time to give birth and a time to die; A time to plant and a time to uproot what is planted. A time to kill and a time to heal; A time to tear down and a time to build up. A time to weep and a time to laugh; A time to mourn and a time to dance; A time to throw stones and a time to gather stones; A time to embrace and a time to shun embracing. A time to search and a time to give up as lost; A time to keep and a time to throw away. A time to tear apart and a time to sew together; A time to be silent and a time to speak. A time to love

and a time to hate; A time for war and a time for peace.

> Ecclesiastes 3:1–8

Ecclesiastes 3:11 continues: "He has made everything appropriate in its time. He has also set eternity in their heart, yet so that man will not find out the work which God has done from the beginning even to the end."

Your life may seem hectic and nonsensical. You may feel like Dorothy from the Wizard of Oz, caught up in that tornado, spinning and twirling about, with no purposeful location or explanation in sight. But it doesn't matter. It's all about the Lord's timing.

Our perceived chaos is the Lord's perfect path.

THE ONLY WAY

The Bible isn't a la carte, that is, you don't just pick and choose what you want to believe. If the Bible says it, that settles it. The Bible is the actual words of God, alive and teeming with hope, salvation, and wisdom.

In the Old Testament, the Lord created rules to live by, known as the Ten Commandments. Every human being, except for Jesus, who never sinned, is sinful in nature. We all fall short of God's glory. But thanks to the shedding of the blood of Jesus Christ in the New Testament, we are forgiven of our sins and will live in eternity with Christ when we die. Christ became the sacrificial lamb because of his love for us. Because of our sinful nature, we could never appear before the holy and righteous Lord on judgment day unless washed of our sins. He enabled us to be righteous in God's eyes. Christians aren't perfect, but we are saved.

Wait. Did I just hear someone say that he is sinless? That he is good and righteous without Christ? I believe I did. Hmm.

Have you ever lied? Have you ever exaggerated about anything?

Have you ever stolen anything? Even a pen or paper clip from work?

Have you ever coveted, that is, wanted what someone else has? His house, wife, lifestyle, appearance, job, or car?

Have you ever committed murder or adultery in your heart? Lusted after a woman or man you saw at the mall, in class, or in a movie? Hated someone for something he did to you or because of the way he looked?

Of course you have; we all have. In my life, I've broken every one of the Ten Commandments. That's why I thank Jesus so very, very much for dying on the cross for me. With my limited human capacities, I really can't fathom what he did for me, but I try to give thanks as best I know how.

Beginning with John 8:1, a woman is caught in the act of adultery. The people wanted to stone her. They took her before Jesus to test him. Jesus then stooped down and wrote something on the ground with his finger. Nobody is certain what Jesus wrote. He possibly may have written the Ten Commandments or written down the many sins of each individual present.

John 8:7 says, "And said to them, 'He who is without sin among you, let him be the first to throw a stone at her.'" He then wrote on the ground again. The accusers then slowly left one by one. No stones were thrown. How could they? Jesus proved to them that they were all sinners too.

I can just visualize each person present with stones in hand, rearing back and getting ready to throw as hard as possible at the woman. However, upon reading what Jesus wrote, they lowered their arms and slowly dropped their stones. *Plunk. Plunk. Plunk.* Then they lowered their sinful heads, turned, and shamefully walked away.

I recall as a youth stealing. I used to say, "What's wrong with that? I was just a kid. I didn't know any better." Yes, I was young, but that goes to show my sinful nature. I never would have stolen, regardless of age, if I didn't have a sinful nature.

To this day, I remember some of the things I stole. I still feel bad about it even though as an adult I prayed and received forgiveness. Isn't it funny how the Lord forgives us for a sin and then forgets about it, but we don't forget and hold onto the guilt long, long after the incident? I remember stealing a toy rubber motorcycle from church. Gasp! Yep, from a church. I was probably around five years old and can still picture that motorcycle. It was about the size of a child's hand, red, and had black, rotating tires. I was at church with my parents and just had to have it, so I stuck it in my pocket.

I also remember stealing firecrackers and stickers from friends. Boy, I had some sticky fingers back then! The reason I'm confiding in my life of crime is to demonstrate that we all have a sinful nature and desperately need Christ in our lives. Why do we need Christ? Maybe some should sit down for this one. Because if you are not born again, if Christ isn't your Lord and Savior, then you will spend an eternity away from him in the pit of hell.

> For God so loved the world, that he gave his only begotten Son, that whoever believes in him shall not perish, but have eternal life. For God did not send the son into the world to judge the world, but that the world might be saved through him. He who believes in him is not judged; he who does not believe has been judged already, because he has not believed in the name of the only begotten Son of God.
>
> John 3:16–18

Remember, we don't just pick and choose what we want to believe when reading the Bible. If you are a servant and steward of Jesus Christ, then you must believe all it says, not just the feel-good, warm, and fuzzy things. The trend with many churches nowadays is to preach only the messages of miracles, healing, and rah-rah, positive types of sermons. I enjoy those too a lot, but there is much more to the Bible. Some purposely won't talk about the devil, hell, and sinning because they don't want to offend anyone. They don't want to lose members. They don't want to lose hearing the sound of *clink* in the collection plate.

But what is more important? Offending someone or not offending and giving him or her a first-class ticket to the hot seat in hell for all eternity?

But what is hell? Quite simply, it's the opposite of heaven. It's being apart and completely disconnected from Christ. If heaven is eternal bliss, incessant joy, and constant comfort, then hell is eternal, unrelenting torture, unbearable heat, and excruciating pain. You can't get away from the torture, as it consumes you twenty-four hours a day forever.

Yes, I think I'd rather offend someone than let him or her endure that. Hell is frightening beyond comprehension and needs to be taken very seriously.

John 5:24 says, "Truly, truly, I say to you, he who hears My word, and believes him who sent Me, has eternal life, and does not come into judgment, but has passed out of death into life."

Do you want life, which is eternity in heaven with Jesus, or death, which is eternity in hell with the devil and his torturers? The choice is yours.

John 8:23–24 continues, "You are from below, I am from above; you are of this world, I am not of this world. Therefore I said to you that you will die in your sins; for unless you believe that I am He, you will die in your sins."

Not too warm and fuzzy, is it?

> If God were your Father, you would love Me, for I proceeded forth and have come from God, for I have not even come on My own initiative, but he sent Me. Why do you not understand what I am saying? It is because you cannot hear My word. You are of your father the devil, and you want to do the desires of your father. He was a murderer from the beginning, and does not stand in the truth because there is no truth in him. Whenever he speaks a lie, he speaks from his own nature, for he is a liar and the father of lies. But because I speak the truth, you do not believe Me. Which one of you convicts Me of sin? If I speak truth, why do you not believe Me? He who is of God hears the words of God; for this reason you do not hear them, because you are not of God.
>
> John 8:42–47

He continues in John 10:10 by referring to the devil as a thief. "The thief comes only to steal and kill and destroy; I came that they may have life, and have it abundantly."

I've heard some people say that Christianity is just

a crutch for weak people, that the truly strong don't need Christ. To that I respond that Christianity isn't a playground or a picnic on a cool, autumn day but instead a battlefield, a battlefield for warriors who constantly battle unrelenting satanic attacks. Once a person becomes a Christian, he must bear the heavy and bulky cross, just like Jesus did. He will be attacked not only by satanic forces in the netherworld but also by his fellow man.

> If the world hates you, you know that it has hated Me before it hated you. If you were of the world, the world would love its own; but because you are not of the world, but I chose you out of the world, because of this the world hates you. Remember the word that I said to you, "A slave is not greater than his master." If they persecuted Me, they will also persecute you; if they kept My word, they will keep yours also.
>
> John 15:18–20

Matthew 10:22 says, "You will be hated by all because of My name, but it is the one who has endured to the end who will be saved."

Being a Christian is very difficult and costly. But it's well worth the price, as it's the only way.

> Then Jesus said to his disciples, "If anyone wishes to come after Me, he must deny himself, and take up his cross and follow Me. For whoever wishes to save his life will lose it; but whoever loses his life for My sake will find it. For what will it profit a man if he gains the whole world and forfeits his soul? Or what will a man give in exchange for his soul? For the Son of Man is going to come in the glory of his Father with his angels, and will then repay every man according to his deeds."
>
> Matthew 16:24–27

To be saved, one needs to be born again and baptized. But what does born again mean? A person is first born into the earthly realm through his human mother. When you accept Christ as your Lord and Savior, you are born a second time, born again, but this time into the spiritual and heavenly realm. You are born again through the Holy Spirit.

John 3:3–7 says, "Truly, truly, I say to you, unless one is born again he cannot see the kingdom of God … unless one is born of water and the Spirit he cannot enter into the kingdom of God … You must be born again."

That means that if you are not born again, hell awaits.

Getting baptized is an official ceremony that allows the Holy Spirit to enter your body. You also are forgiven of sins at that time and will spend everlasting life in heaven. I was baptized as an infant and to this day, still have my silver baptismal cup. However, I got baptized again at the age of forty-five, that time as a free-thinking adult. I wanted to show my seriousness about serving the Lord and to ensure that the Holy Spirit truly is with me.

John 14:6 says, "I am the way, and the truth, and the life; no one comes to the Father but through Me."

That means that if you are not born again, hell awaits.

God will never force anyone to become a Christian. He's given you freedom of choice. You may worship what and whom you want. If you want to worship a mosquito, you are entitled, as that's freedom of choice. However, choose wisely.

John 6:47 says, "Truly, truly, I say to you, he who believes has eternal life."

To me, the choice is obvious.

A FINAL THOUGHT

Do you have so many problems that you feel overwhelmed? Do you lack courage and strength or feel weak and worthless? Are you lonely or filled with anxiety? Do you think that you are an average or even below average individual who could never serve the Lord in any way?

If so, rejoice! The Lord wants and needs someone just like you. He uses average, ordinary, problem-laden folks, just like you and me. Not perfect people, because there are none.

He used a shepherd boy named David to kill the giant Goliath.

He used Jonah, a fear-laden man who would rather drown than be obedient, to save a city.

He used Moses, a murderer with a speech impediment, to save the children of Israel.

He used Joseph, a man thrown into a pit and sold to slavery, to save Egypt during a famine.

Although faced with huge obstacles and roadblocks,

they all had one vital ingredient in common: the Lord. They never would have succeeded without the Lord. For success is merely understanding and then fulfilling the Lord's purpose for your life.

So don't think you can't because you can. Don't think you are unable because you are able. Don't think you don't have what it takes because you do have what it takes.

Just follow Norman Vincent Peale's advice: "Dream creative dreams. Set high and worthwhile goals. Take the first decisive step toward your goal. Then take another step, and another, and another, until the goal is reached, the ambition realized, the mission accomplished. No matter how long it takes, persist. No matter how discouraged you get, persevere. No matter how much you want to quit, hang in there."

Hope. Dream. Believe. And you will accomplish marvelous things. But don't forget the most important and necessary ingredient: put on the full armor of God.

> Finally, be strong in the Lord and in the strength of his might. Put on the full armor of God, so that you will be able to stand firm against the schemes of the devil. For our struggle is not against flesh and blood, but against the rulers, against the powers, against the world forces of this darkness, against the spiritual forces of wickedness in the

heavenly places. Therefore, take up the full armor of God, so that you will be able to resist in the evil day, and having done everything, to stand firm. Stand firm therefore, having girded your loins with truth, and having put on the breastplate of righteousness, and having shod your feet with the preparation of the gospel of peace; in addition to all, taking up the shield of faith with which you will be able to extinguish all the flaming arrows of the evil one. And take the helmet of salvation, and the sword of the Spirit, which is the word of God.

Ephesians 6:10–17